A NATURE POEM FOR EVERY AUTUMN EVENING

A NATURE POEM FOR EVERY AUTUMN EVENING

EDITED BY *Jane McMorland Hunter*

ILLUSTRATIONS BY *Jessamy Hawke*

BATSFORD

First published in the United Kingdom
in 2024 by
Batsford
43 Great Ormond Street
London
WC1N 3HZ

An imprint of B. T. Batsford Holdings Limited

ISBN 978 1 84994 862 3

A CIP catalogue record for this book is available from the
British Library.

10 9 8 7 6 5 4 3 2 1

Reproduction by Rival Colour Ltd, UK
Printed and bound in Turkey by Elma Basim

This book can be ordered direct from the publisher at
www.batsfordbooks.com, or try your local bookshop

Illustrations by Jessamy Hawke

MIX
From well-
managed forests
FSC
www.fsc.org FSC® C164814

CONTENTS

To Matilda, who came home. And to Mat and Sarah, who helped. With all my love.

ABOUT THE EDITOR

Jane McMorland Hunter has compiled many anthologies of poetry for Batsford and the National Trust. She also writes gardening and cookery books and works as a gardener and at Hatchards bookshop in Piccadilly. She lives in London with a small, grey tabby cat.

Introduction

After the long summer months, autumn is a
time to seize the moment and enjoy the natural
world as much as possible before winter sets in.
Whether basking in the last of the sunshine or
sitting by a roaring fire, autumn evenings are
a perfect time to enjoy a poem. Darkness may
arrive earlier in the day but that need not stop
the enjoyment of a poem a day. The poets here
span over four hundred years and describe every
aspect of the natural world in autumn from trees
to birds and sea to sky.

The start of autumn is often the gentlest
time of the year, with warm days, sunlit
evenings and soft breezes. The opening line of
John Keats' poem with the phrase 'mists and
mellow fruitfulness' is justly renowned, as is
Amy Lowell's 'Tang of fruitage in the air,' and
'Warmth of earth'. Both poets portray a mild and
plentiful time, for as well as being gentle, the
start of autumn is also a time of abundance in
nature, with harvests for humans, animals and
birds. In our modern world of convenience and

year-round availability, it is easy to overlook the fact that this abundance is a preparation for the hardships and cold of the late autumn and winter to come. Arthur Hugh Clough describes the time as 'soft September' but there are changes in the air, imperceptible at first, hastening as the season progresses towards the solemn wind and solemn rain of Katherine Mansfield. Even amidst the golden fields and sagging orchards Rachel Field notices something that whispers 'Snow' and a quiet voice cautions 'Frost'. Then the wild west wind of Shelley's verse comes, harrying the leaves and winged seeds, destroying and preserving at the same time.

Every season has its own range of colours, and autumn is the moment for the trees. This is the time when they come to the fore, either staining the world red and gold or remaining as bastions of green right through into winter and beyond to the following spring. The dark green of summer fades and, as autumn progresses, so the reds and golds of the falling leaves deepen and intensify. For John Drinkwater, the leaves spinning down to earth 'rich apparelled in decay' are more beautiful in death than they were in life. As the leaf cover thins the sunlight reaches the ground beneath the trees, giving a range of colours not seen in such glory since the previous autumn; bright patches of sunlight contrasting with deep shade which spreads as the sun sinks. This also is a time of dappled light and shadows, much beloved by John Davidson and Gerard Manley Hopkins. Which leads us to evening, as autumn is very much the evening of the year.

'Twilight' is one of my favourite words in the English language, conjuring up visions of that magical time between day and night, when the shadows lengthen, edges are blurred and light and dark merge. In the words of Samuel Palmer it is a time of trembling light and, one of my favourite poets, Sara Teasdale, describes the change perfectly; 'The stately tragedy of dusk/ Drew to its perfect close'. The moon and stars follow, appearing earlier as the season progresses. This is one of the benefits of the nights drawing in; on a quiet evening one can read of George Macdonald's bright-eyed moon, or Walter de la Mare's silvery one and see the real thing through the windows.

For some poets the evening of the year is linked with the evening of life; spring is the season of youth and growth, autumn of age and maturity. Leaves underfoot have a scent of death and, for all its brilliance, we know that much of the natural world is closing down. In contrast, perhaps surprisingly, now is the time that many poets to turn to the sea. Buckets and spades are gone and one can appreciate the ocean's grandeur. Storm or calm alike, the sea has the power to enchant us. Romantic legends of fantastic journeys, sheer miracles of loveliness and the perfection of a single shell (Henry Wadsworth Longfellow, Christina Rossetti and Mary Webb, should you wish to read the entire poem) describe its many wonders.

Poetry can take liberties regarding climate change, global warming and seasonal inconsistencies. Here, in verse, autumn arrives on time, bridging the gap between summer and winter with all the timely delights we would want. I hope this collection does justice to its delights: atmospheric, beautiful and slightly mysterious.

> Something told the wild geese
> > It was time to fly, -
> Summer sun was on their wings,
> > Winter in their cry.

(From 'Something Told the Wild Geese' by Rachel Field)

SEPTEMBER

Colder Airs Creeping from the Misty Moon

1ˢᵀ SEPTEMBER

Autumn

FROM *THE LAND*

Now I have told the year from dawn to dusk,
Its morning and its evening and its noon;
Once round the sun our slanting orbit rolled,
Four times the seasons changed, thirteen the moon;
Corn grew from seed to husk,
The young spring grass for provender for herds;
Drought came, and earth was grateful for the rain;
The bees streamed in and out the summer hives;
Birds wildly sang; were silent; birds
With summer's passing fitfully sang again;
The loaded waggon crossed the field; the sea
Spread her great generous pasture as a robe
Whereon the slow ships, circling statelily,
Are patterned round the globe.

Vita Sackville-West (1892–1962)

2ND SEPTEMBER

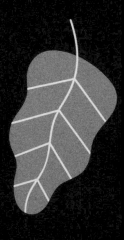

Autumn Song

Autumn clouds are flying, flying
   O'er the waste of blue;
Summer flowers are dying, dying,
   Late so lovely new.
Labouring wains are slowly rolling
   Home with winter grain;
Holy bells are slowly tolling
   Over buried men.

Goldener light sets noon a sleeping
   Like an afternoon;
Colder airs come stealing, creeping
   From the misty moon;
And the leaves, of old age dying,
   Earthy hues put on;
Out on every lone wind sighing
   That their day is gone.

Autumn's sun is sinking, sinking
   Down to winter low;
And our hearts are thinking, thinking
   Of the sleet and snow;
For our sun is slowly sliding
   Down the hill of might;

And no moon is softly gliding
   Up the slope of night.

See the bare fields' pillaged prizes
   Heaped in golden glooms!
See, the earth's outworn sunrises
   Dream in cloudy tombs!
Darkling flowers but wait the blowing
   Of a quickening wind;
And the man, through Death's door going,
   Leaves old Death behind.

Mourn not, then, clear tones that alter;
   Let the gold turn gray;
Feet, though feeble, still may falter
   Toward the better day!
Brother, let not weak faith linger
   O'er a withered thing;
Mark how Autumn's prophet finger
   Burns to hues of Spring.

George MacDonald (1824–1905)

3RD SEPTEMBER

Autumn

Autumn comes laden with her ripened load
Of fruitage and so scatters them abroad
That each fern smothered heath and molehill waste
Are black with bramble berrys – where in haste
The chubby urchins from the village hie
To feast them there stained with the purple dye
While painted woods around my rambles be
In draperies worthy of eternity
Yet will the leaves soon patter on the ground
And deaths deaf voice awake at every sound
One drops – then others – and the last that fell
Rings for those left behind their passing bell
Thus memory every where her tidings brings
How sad death robs us of lifes dearest things

John Clare (1793–1864)

4TH SEPTEMBER

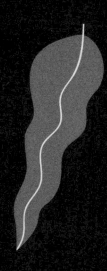

To Autumn

I

Season of mists and mellow fruitfulness,
  Close bosom-friend of the maturing sun;
Conspiring with him how to load and bless
  With fruit the vines that round the thatch-eves run;
To bend with apples the moss'd cottage-trees,
  And fill all fruit with ripeness to the core;
    To swell the gourd, and plump, the hazel shells
  With a sweet kernel; to set budding more,
And still more, later flowers for the bees,
Until they think warm days will never cease,
  For Summer has o'er-brimmed their clammy cells.

II

Who hath not seen thee oft amid thy store?
  Sometimes whoever seeks abroad may find
Thee sitting careless on a granary floor,
  Thy hair soft-lifted by the winnowing wind;
Or on a half-reap'd furrow sound asleep,
  Drows'd with the fume of poppies, while thy hook
    Spares the next swathe and all its twined flowers:
And sometimes like a gleaner thou dost keep
  Steady thy laden head across a brook;
  Or by a cyder-press, with patient look,
    Thou watchest the last oozing hours by hours.

III

Where are the songs of Spring? Ay, where are they?
    Think not of them, thou hast thy music too, –
While barred clouds bloom the soft-dying day,
    And touch the stubble-plains with rosy hue;
Then in a wilful choir the small gnats mourn
    Among the river sallows, borne aloft
        Or sinking as the light wind lives or dies;
And full-grown lambs loud bleat from hilly bourn;
    Hedge-crickets sing; and now with treble soft
    The red-breast whistles from a garden-croft;
        And gathering swallows twitter in the skies.

John Keats (1795–1821)

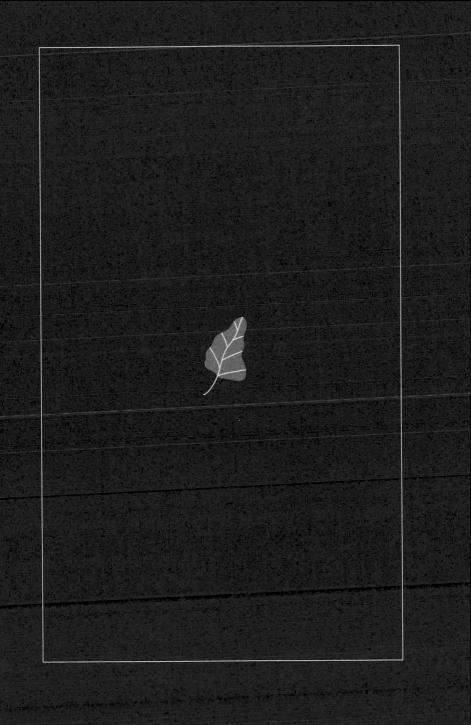

5TH SEPTEMBER

5TH SEPTEMBER

September Day

(PONT DE NEUILLY)

The Seine flows out of the mist
   And into the mist again;
The trees lean over the water,
   The small leaves fall like rain.

The leaves fall patiently,
   Nothing remembers or grieves;
The river takes to the sea
   The yellow drift of the leaves.

Milky and cold is the air,
   The leaves float with the stream,
The river comes out of a sleep
   And goes away in a dream.

Sara Teasdale (1884–1933)

6TH SEPTEMBER

Binsey Poplars

FELLED 1879

My aspens dear, whose airy cages quelled,
Quelled or quenched in leaves the leaping sun,
Áll félled, félled, are áll félled;
Of a fresh and following folded rank
Not spared, not one
That dandled a sandalled
Shadow that swam or sank
On meadow and river and wind-wandering weed
winding bank.

O if we but knew what we do
When we delve or hew –
Hack and rack the growing green!
Since Country is so tender
To tóuch, her béing só slénder,
That, like this sleek and seeing ball
But a prick will make no eye at all,
Where we, even where we mean
To mend her we end her,
When we hew or delve:

After-comers cannot guess the beauty been.
    Ten or twelve, only ten or twelve
        Strokes of havoc unselve
            The sweet especial scene,
        Rural scene, a rural scene,
        Sweet especial rural scene.

Gerard Manley Hopkins (1844–1889)

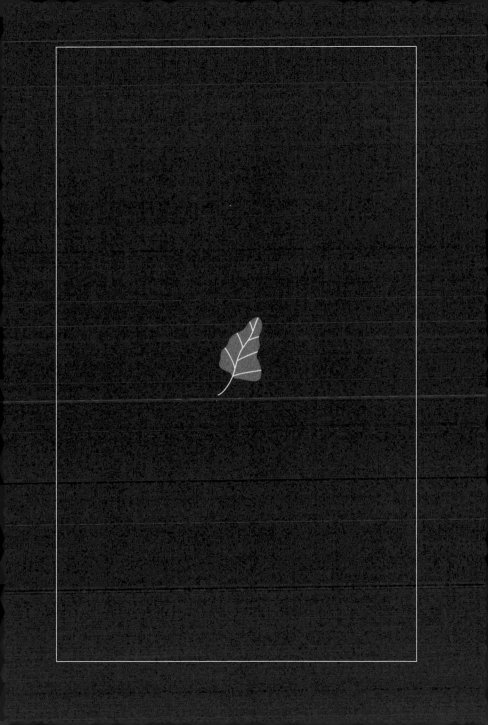

7TH SEPTEMBER

When Soft September Brings Again

When soft September brings again
  To yonder gorse its golden glow,
And Snowdon sends its autumn rain
  To bid thy current livelier flow;
Amid that ashen foliage light
When scarlet beads are glistering bright,
While alder boughs unchanged are seen
In summer livery of green;
When clouds before the cooler breeze
Are flying, white and large; with these
Returning, so I may return,
And find thee changeless, Pont-y-wern.

Arthur Hugh Clough (1819–1861)

8TH SEPTEMBER

The Deserted Garden

VERSES 1–6

I mind me in the days departed,
How often underneath the sun
With childish bounds I used to run
   To a garden long deserted.

The beds and walks were vanished quite;
And wheresoe'er had struck the spade,
The greenest grasses Nature laid,
   To sanctify her right.

I called the place my wilderness,
For no one entered there but I;
The sheep looked in, the grass to espy,
   And passed it ne'ertheless.

The trees were interwoven wild,
And spread their boughs enough about
To keep both sheep and shepherd out,
   But not a happy child.

Adventurous joy it was for me!
I crept beneath the boughs, and found
A circle smooth of mossy ground
  Beneath a poplar tree.

Old garden rose-trees hedged it in,
Bedropt with roses waxen-white,
Well satisfied with dew and light,
  And careless to be seen.

Elizabeth Barrett Browning (1806–1861)

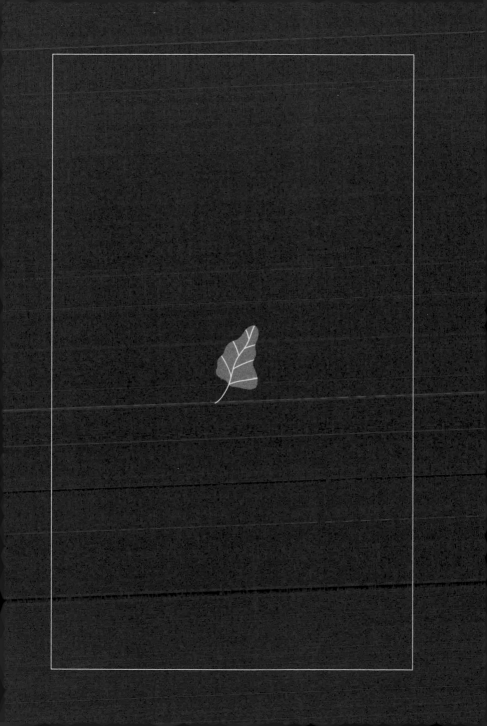

9ᵀᴴ SEPTEMBER

Ode to the West Wind

PART I

O wild West Wind, thou breath of Autumn's being,
Thou, from whose unseen presence the leaves dead
Are driven, like ghosts from an enchanter fleeing,

Yellow, and black, and pale, and hectic red,
Pestilence-stricken multitudes: O thou,
Who chariotest to their dark wintry bed

The wingèd seeds, where they lie cold and low,
Each like a corpse within its grave, until
Thine azure sister of the Spring shall blow

Her clarion o'er the dreaming earth, and fill
(Driving sweet buds like flocks to feed in air)
With living hues and odours plain and hill:

Wild Spirit, which art moving everywhere;
Destroyer and preserver; hear, oh, hear!

Percy Bysshe Shelley (1792–1822)

10TH SEPTEMBER

Autumn

All day I have watched the purple vine leaves
Fall into the water.
And now in the moonlight they still fall,
But each leaf is fringed with silver.

Amy Lowell (1874–1925)

11TH SEPTEMBER

Twilight Time

LINES 1–24

And now the trembling light
Glimmers behind the little hills and corn,
Lingering as loath to part. Yet part thou must,
And though than open day far pleasing more
(Ere yet the fields and pearlèd cups of flowers
    Twinkle in the parting light),
Thee night shall hide, sweet visionary gleam
That softly lookest through the rising dew –
    Till, all like silver bright.
The Faithful Witness, pure and white
Shall look o'er yonder grassy hill,
  At this village, safe and still.
  All is safe and all is still,
Save what noise the watch-dog makes
  Or the shrill cock the silence breaks
  Now and then –
  And now and then –
  Hark! once again,
  The wether's bell to us doth tell
  Some little stirring in the fold.
  Methinks the lingering, dying ray
    Of twilight time doth seem more fair.

Samuel Palmer (1805–1863)

12TH SEPTEMBER

Remembrance of Nature

Oh Nature thou didst rear me for thine own,
With thy free singing-birds and mountain-brooks,
Feeding my thoughts in primrose-haunted nooks
With fairy fantasies and wood-dreams lone;
And thou didst teach me every wandering tone
Drawn from thy many-whispering trees and waves,
And guide my steps to founts and sparry caves,
And where bright mosses wove thee a rich throne
Midst the green hills. And now that, far estranged
From all sweet sounds and odours of thy breath,
Fading I lie, within my heart unchanged
So glows the love of thee that not for death
Seems that pure passion's fervour, but ordained
To meet on brighter shores thy majesty unstained.

Felicia Hemans (1793–1835)

13ᵀᴴ SEPTEMBER

Something Told the Wild Geese

Something told the wild geese
  It was time to go.
Though the fields lay golden
  Something whispered, – 'Snow.'
Leaves were green and stirring,
  Berries, luster-glossed,
But beneath warm feathers
  Something cautioned, – 'Frost.'
All the sagging orchards
  Steamed with amber spice,
But each wild breast stiffened
  At remembered ice.
Something told the wild geese
  It was time to fly, –
Summer sun was on their wings,
  Winter in their cry.

Rachel Field (1894–1942)

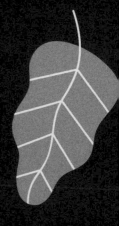

14TH SEPTEMBER

September

The dark green Summer, with its massive hues.
Fades into Autumn's tincture manifold.
A gorgeous garniture of fire and gold
The high slope of the ferny hill indues.
The mists of morn in slumbering layers diffuse
O'er glimmering rock, smooth lake, and spiked array
Of hedge-row thorns, a unity of grey.
All things appear their tangible form to lose
In ghostly vastness. But anon the gloom
Melts, as the Sun puts off his muddy veil;
And now the birds their twittering songs resume.
All Summer silent in the leafy dale.
In Spring they piped of love on every tree.
But now they sing the song of memory.

Hartley Coleridge (1796–1849)

15TH SEPTEMBER

The Road Not Taken

Two roads diverged in a yellow wood,
And sorry I could not travel both
And be one traveller, long I stood
And looked down one as far as I could
To where it bent in the undergrowth;

Then took the other, as just as fair,
And having perhaps the better claim,
Because it was grassy and wanted wear;
Though as for that the passing there
Had worn them really about the same,

And both that morning equally lay
In leaves no step had trodden black.
Oh, I kept the first for another day!
Yet knowing how way leads on to way,
I doubted if I should ever come back.

I shall be telling this with a sigh
Somewhere ages and ages hence:
Two roads diverged in a wood, and I –
I took the one less travelled by,
And that has made all the difference.

Robert Frost (1874–1963)

16TH SEPTEMBER

Sudden Shower

Black grows the southern clouds betokening rain
And humming hive bees homeward hurry bye
They feel the change – so let us shun the grain
And take the broad road while our feet are dry
Aye there some dropples moistened in my face
And pattered on my hat – tis coming nigh
Lets look about and find a sheltering place
The little things around like you and I
Are hurrying thro the grass to shun the shower
Here stoops an Ash tree – hark the wind gets high
But never mind its Ivy for an hour
Rain as it may will keep us dryly here
That little Wren knows well his sheltering bower
Nor leaves his dry house tho we come so near

John Clare (1793–1864)

17TH SEPTEMBER

Songs of the Autumn Nights

SONG I

O night, send up the harvest moon
  To walk about the fields,
And make of midnight magic noon
  On lonely tarns and wealds.

In golden ranks, with golden crowns,
  All in the yellow land,
Old solemn kings in rustling gowns,
  The shocks moon-charmed stand.

Sky-mirror she, afloat in space,
  Beholds our coming morn:
Her heavenly joy hath such a grace,
  It ripens earthly corn;

Like some lone saint with upward eyes,
  Lost in the deeps of prayer:
The people still their prayers and sighs,
  And gazing ripen there.

George MacDonald (1824–1905)

18ᵀᴴ SEPTEMBER

The Autumn Crocus

In the high woods that crest our hills,
Upon a steep, rough slope of forest ground,
Where few flowers grow, sweet blooms today I found
Of the Autumn Crocus, blowing pale and fair.
Dim falls the sunlight there;
And a mild fragrance the lone thicket fills.

Languidly curved, the long white stems
Their purple flowers' gold treasure scarce display:
Lost were their leaves since in the distant spring,
Their February sisters showed so gay.
Roses of June, ye too have followed fleet!
Forsaken now, and shaded as by thought,
As by the human shade of thought and dreams,
They bloom 'mid the dark wood, whose air has wrought
With what soft nights and mornings of still dew!
Into their slender petals that clear hue,
Like paleness in fresh cheeks; a thing
On earth, I vowed, ne'er grew
More delicately pure, more shyly sweet.
Child of the pensive autumn woods!
So lovely, though thou dwell obscure and lone,
And though thy flush and gaiety be gone;
Say, among flowers of the sad, human mind,
Where shall I ever find
So rare a grace? in what shy solitudes?

Laurence Binyon (1869–1943)

19TH SEPTEMBER

On Esthwaite Water

VERSES 1–4

O'er Esthwaite's lake, serene and still,
   At sunset's silent peaceful hour
Scarce moved the zephyr's softest breath,
   Or sighed along its reedy shore.

The lovely landscape on its sides,
   With evening's softening hues impressed,
Shared in the general calm, and gave
   Sweet visions of repose and rest.

Inverted on the waveless flood,
   A spotless mirror smooth and clear,
Each fair surrounding object shone
   In softer beauty imaged there.

Brown hills and woods of various shades,
   Orchards and sloping meadows green,
Sweet rural seats and sheltered farms,
   Were in the bright reflector seen.

Isabella Lickbarrow (1784–1847)

20TH SEPTEMBER

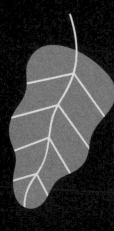

Apple-Trees

When autumn stains and dapples
The diverse land,
Thickly studded with apples
The apple-trees stand.

Their mystery none discovers,
So none can tell –
Not the most passionate lovers
Of garth and fell;
For the silent sunlight weaves
The orchard spell,
Bough, bole, and root,
Mysterious, hung with leaves,
Embossed with fruit.

Though merle and throstle were loud,
Silent their passion in spring,
A blush of blossom wild-scented;
And now when no song-birds sing.
They are heavy with apples and proud
And supremely contented –
All fertile and green and sappy,
No wish denied,
Exceedingly quiet and happy
And satisfied!

No jealousy, anger, or fashion
Of strife
Perturbs in their stations
The apple-trees. Life
Is an effortless passion,
Fruit, bough, and stem,
A beautiful patience
For them.

Frost of the harvest-moon
Changes their sap to wine;
Ruddy and golden soon
Their clustered orbs will shine,
By favour
Of many a wind,
Of morn and noon and night,
Fulfilled from core to rind
With savour
Of all delight.

John Davidson (1857–1909)

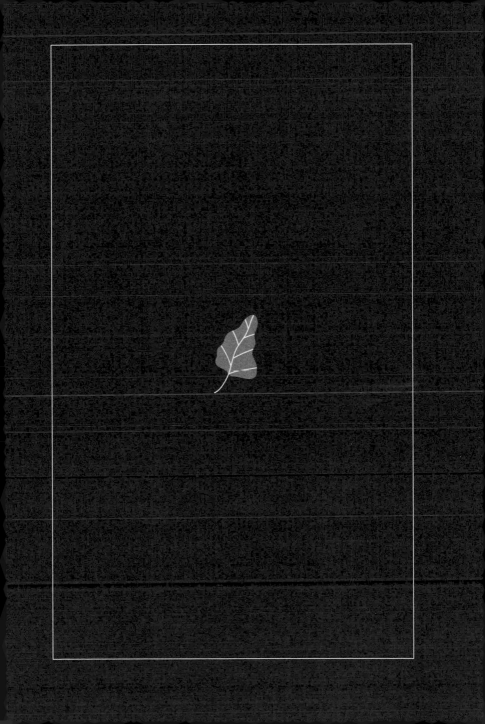

21ˢᵀ SEPTEMBER

Pied Beauty

Glory be to God for dappled things –
    For skies of couple-colour as a brinded cow;
  For rose-moles all in stipple upon trout that swim;
Fresh-firecoal chestnut-falls; finches' wings;
  Landscape plotted and pieced – fold, fallow, and plough;
  And áll trades, their gear and tackle and trim.

All things counter, original, spáre, strange;
  Whatever is fickle, frecklèd (who knows how?)
    With swíft, slów; sweet, sóur; adázzle, dím;
He fathers-forth whose beauty is pást change:
                Práise him.

Gerard Manley Hopkins (1844–1889)

22ND SEPTEMBER

The Harvest Moon

The flame-red moon, the harvest moon,
Rolls along the hills, gently bouncing,
A vast balloon,
Till it takes off, and sinks upward
To lie in the bottom of the sky, like a gold doubloon.

The harvest moon has come,
Booming softly through heaven, like a bassoon.
And earth replies all night, like a deep drum.

So people can't sleep,
So they go out where elms and oak trees keep
A kneeling vigil, in a religious hush.
The harvest moon has come!

And all the moonlit cows and all the sheep
Stare up at her petrified, while she swells
Filling heaven, as if red hot, and sailing
Closer and closer like the end of the world.

Till the gold fields of stiff wheat
Cry 'We are ripe, reap us!' and the rivers
Sweat from the melting hills.

Ted Hughes (1930–1998)

23ᴿᴰ SEPTEMBER

Diary of a Church Mouse

Here among long-discarded cassocks,
Damp stools, and half-split open hassocks,
Here where the Vicar never looks
I nibble through old service books.
Lean and alone I spend my days
Behind this Church of England baize.
I share my dark forgotten room
With two oil-lamps and half a broom.
The cleaner never bothers me,
So here I eat my frugal tea.
My bread is sawdust mixed with straw;
My jam is polish for the floor.
Christmas and Easter may be feasts
For congregations and for priests,
And so may Whitsun. All the same,
They do not fill my meagre frame.
For me the only feast at all
Is Autumn's Harvest Festival,
When I can satisfy my want
With ears of corn around the font.
I climb the eagle's brazen head
To burrow through a loaf of bread.
I scramble up the pulpit stair

And gnaw the marrows hanging there.
It is enjoyable to taste
These items ere they go to waste,
But how annoying when one finds
That other mice with pagan minds
Come into church my food to share
Who have no proper business there.
Two field mice who have no desire
To be baptized, invade the choir.
A large and most unfriendly rat
Comes in to see what we are at.
He says he thinks there is no God
And yet he comes ... it's rather odd.
This year he stole a sheaf of wheat
(It screened our special preacher's seat),
And prosperous mice from fields away
Come in to hear our organ play,
And under cover of its notes
Ate through the altar's sheaf of oats.
A Low Church mouse, who thinks that I

Am too papistical, and High,
Yet somehow doesn't think it wrong
To munch through Harvest Evensong,
While I, who starve the whole year through,
Must share my food with rodents who
Except at this time of the year
Not once inside the church appear.
Within the human world I know
Such goings-on could not be so,
For human beings only do
What their religion tells them to.
They read the Bible every day
And always, night and morning, pray,
And just like me, the good church mouse,
Worship each week in God's own house,
But all the same it's strange to me
How very full the church can be
With people I don't see at all
Except at Harvest Festival.

John Betjeman (1906–1984)

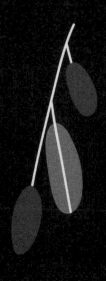

24TH SEPTEMBER

The Owl

When cats run home and light is come,
  And dew is cold upon the ground,
And the far-off stream is dumb,
  And the whirring sail goes round,
  And the whirring sail goes round;
    Alone and warming his five wits,
    The white owl in the belfry sits.

When merry milkmaids click the latch,
  And rarely smells the new-mown hay,
And the cock hath sung beneath the thatch
  Twice or thrice his roundelay,
  Twice or thrice his roundelay;
    Alone and warming his five wits,
    The white owl in the belfry sits.

Alfred, Lord Tennyson (1809–1892)

25TH SEPTEMBER

The Solitary Reaper

Behold her, single in the field,
Yon solitary Highland Lass!
Reaping and singing by herself;
Stop here, or gently pass!
Alone she cuts and binds the grain,
And sings a melancholy strain;
O listen! for the Vale profound
Is overflowing with the sound.

No Nightingale did ever chaunt
So sweetly to reposing bands
Of Travellers in some shady haunt,
Among Arabian Sands:
No sweeter voice was ever heard
In spring-time from the Cuckoo-bird,
Breaking the silence of the seas
Among the farthest Hebrides.

Will no one tell me what she sings? –
Perhaps the plaintive numbers flow
For old, unhappy, far-off things,
And battles long ago:
Or is it some more humble lay,
Familiar matter of to-day?
Some natural sorrow, loss, or pain,
That has been, and may be again?

Whate'er the theme, the Maiden sang
As if her song could have no ending;
I saw her singing at her work,
And o'er the sickle bending;
I listened till I had my fill:
And, as I mounted up the hill,
The music in my heart I bore,
Long after it was heard no more.

William Wordsworth (1770–1850)

26TH SEPTEMBER

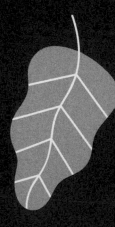

Late September

Tang of fruitage in the air;
Red boughs bursting everywhere;
Shimmering of seeded grass;
Hooded gentians all a'mass.

Warmth of earth, and cloudless wind
Tearing off the husky rind,
Blowing feathered seeds to fall
By the sun-baked, sheltering wall.

Beech trees in a golden haze;
Hardy sumachs all ablaze,
Glowing through the silver birches.
How that pine tree shouts and lurches!

From the sunny door-jamb high,
Swings the shell of a butterfly.
Scrape of insect violins
Through the stubble shrilly dins.

Every blade's a minaret
Where a small muezzin's set,
Loudly calling us to pray
At the miracle of day.

Then the purple-lidded night
Westering comes, her footsteps light
Guided by the radiant boon
Of a sickle-shaped new moon.

Amy Lowell (1874–1925)

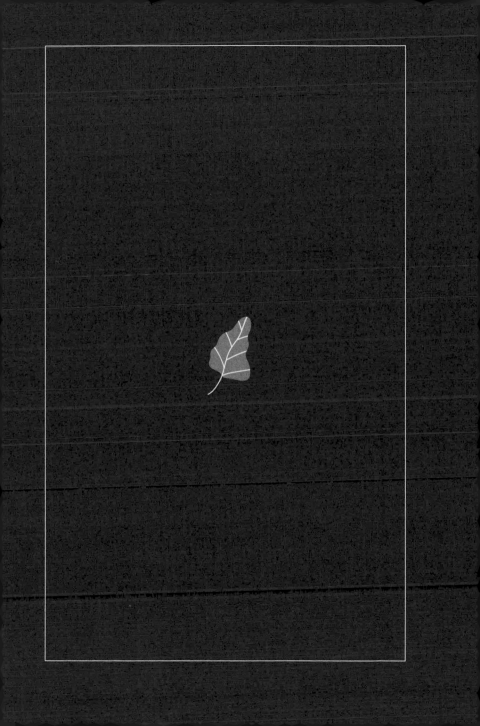

27TH SEPTEMBER

Tell Me Not Here, It Needs Not Saying

LAST POEMS XL

Tell me not here, it needs not saying,
  What tune the enchantress plays
In aftermaths of soft September
  Or under blanching mays,
For she and I were long acquainted
  And I knew all her ways.

On russet floors, by waters idle,
  The pine lets fall its cone;
The cuckoo shouts all day at nothing
  In leafy dells alone;
And traveller's joy beguiles in autumn
  Hearts that have lost their own.

On acres of the seeded grasses
  The changing burnish heaves;
Or marshalled under moons of harvest
  Stand still all night the sheaves;
Or beeches strip in storms for winter
  And stain the wind with leaves.

Possess, as I possessed a season,
    The countries I resign,
Where over elmy plains the highway
    Would mount the hills and shine,
And full of shade the pillared forest
    Would murmur and be mine.

For nature, heartless, witless nature,
    Will neither care nor know
What stranger's feet may find the meadow
    And trespass there and go,
Nor ask amid the dews of morning
    If they are mine or no.

A. E. Housman (1859–1936)

28ᵀᴴ SEPTEMBER

In the Woods

I was in the woods to-day,
  And the leaves were spinning there,
Rich apparelled in decay, –
  In decay more wholly fair
  Than in life they ever were.

Gold and rich barbaric red
  Freakt with pale and sapless vein,
Spinning, spinning, spun and sped
  With a little sob of pain
  Back to harbouring earth again.

Long in homely green they shone
  Through the summer rains and sun,
Now their humbleness is gone,
  Now their little season run,
  Pomp and pageantry begun.

Sweet was life, and buoyant breath,
  Lovely too; but for a day
Issues from the house of death
  Yet more beautiful array:
  Hark, a whisper – 'Come away.'

One by one they spin and fall,
  But they fall in regal pride:
Dying, do they hear a call
  Rising from an ebbless tide,
  And, hearing, are beatified?

John Drinkwater (1882–1937)

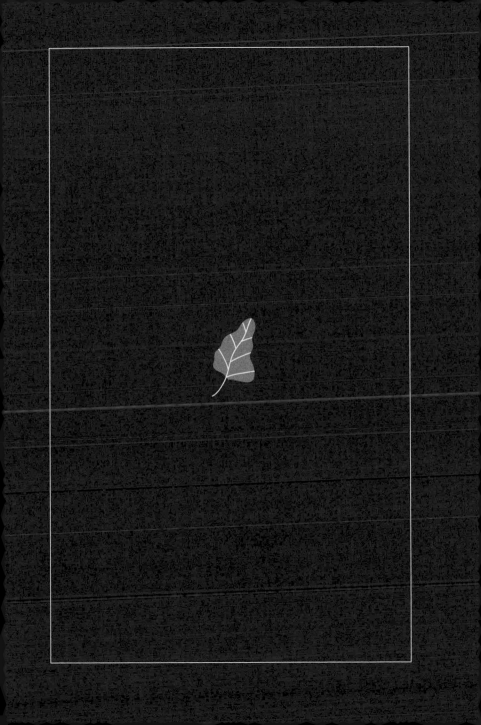

29TH SEPTEMBER

Bavarian Gentians

Not every man has gentians in his house
in Soft September, at slow, Sad Michaelmas.

Bavarian gentians, big and dark, only dark
darkening the daytime torch-like with the smoking
    blueness of Pluto's gloom,
ribbed and torch-like, with their blaze of darkness spread blue
down flattening into points, flattened under the sweep of
    white day
torch-flower of the blue-smoking darkness, Pluto's
    dark-blue daze,
black lamps from the halls of Dis, burning dark blue,
giving off darkness, blue darkness, as Demeter's pale lamps
    give off light,
lead me then, lead me the way.

Reach me a gentian, give me a torch!
let me guide myself with the blue, forked torch of a flower
down the darker and darker stairs, where blue is darkened
    on blueness,
even where Persephone goes, just now, from the frosted
    September
to the sightless realm where darkness is awake upon the dark
and Persephone herself is but a voice
or a darkness invisible enfolded in the deeper dark
of the arms Plutonic, and pierced with the passion of dense
    gloom,
among the splendour of torches of darkness, shedding
    darkness on the lost bride and her groom.

D. H. Lawrence (1885–1930)

30TH SEPTEMBER

Autumn Twilight: Grey and Gold

FROM INTERMEZZO: PASTORAL

The long September evening dies
In mist along the fields and lanes;
Only a few faint stars surprise
The lingering twilight as it wanes.

Night creeps across the darkening vale;
On the horizon tree by tree
Fades into shadowy skies as pale
As moonlight on a shadowy sea.

And, down the mist-enfolded lanes,
Grown pensive now with evening,
See, lingering as the twilight wanes,
Lover with lover wandering.

Arthur Symons (1865–1945)

OCTOBER

The Western Sun Withdraws

1ST OCTOBER

There is a Solemn Wind To-Night

There is a solemn wind to-night
   That sings of solemn rain;
The trees that have been quiet so long
   Flutter and start again.

The slender trees, the heavy trees,
   The fruit trees laden and proud,
Lift up their branches to the wind
   That cries to them so loud.

The little bushes and the plants
   Bow to the solemn sound,
And every tiniest blade of grass
   Shakes on the quiet ground.

Katherine Mansfield (1888–1923)

2ND OCTOBER

Autumn

I saw old Autumn in the misty morn
Stand shadowless like Silence, listening
To silence, for no lonely bird would sing
Into his hollow ear from woods forlorn,
Nor lowly hedge nor solitary thorn; –
Shaking his languid locks all dewy bright
With tangled gossamer that fell by night,
   Pearling his coronet of golden corn.

Where are the songs of Summer? – With the sun,
Oping the dusky eyelids of the south,
Till shade and silence waken up as one,
And Morning sings with a warm odorous mouth.
Where are the merry birds? – Away, away,
On panting wings through the inclement skies,
   Lest owls should prey
   Undazzled at noonday,
And tear with horny beak their lustrous eyes.

Where are the blooms of Summer? – In the west,
Blushing their last to the last sunny hours,
When the mild Eve by sudden Night is prest
Like tearful Proserpine, snatch'd from her flow'rs
    To a most gloomy breast.
Where is the pride of Summer, – the green pine, –
The many, many leaves all twinkling? – Three
    On the moss'd elm; three on the naked lime
Trembling, – and one upon the old oak-tree!
    Where is the Dryad's immortality? –
Gone into mournful cypress and dark yew,
Or wearing the long gloomy Winter through
    In the smooth holly's green eternity.
The squirrel gloats on his accomplish'd hoard,
The ants have brimm'd their garners with ripe grain,
    And honey bees have stor'd
The sweets of Summer in their luscious cells;
The swallows all have wing'd across the main;
But here the Autumn melancholy dwells,
    And sighs her tearful spells
Amongst the sunless shadows of the plain.
    Alone, alone,
    Upon a mossy stone,

She sits and reckons up the dead and gone
With the last leaves for a love-rosary,
Whilst all the wither'd world looks drearily,
Like a dim picture of the drowned past
In the hush'd mind's mysterious far away,
Doubtful what ghostly thing will steal the last
Into that distance, grey upon the grey.
O go and sit with her, and be o'ershaded
Under the languid downfall of her hair:
She wears a coronal of flowers faded
Upon her forehead, and a face of care; –
There is enough of wither'd every where
To make her bower, – and enough of gloom;
There is enough of sadness to invite,
If only for the rose that died, whose doom
Is Beauty's, – she that with the living bloom
Of conscious cheeks most beautifies the light; –
There is enough of sorrowing, and quite
Enough of bitter fruits the earth doth bear, –
Enough of chilly droppings for her bowl;
Enough of fear and shadowy despair,
To frame her cloudy prison for the soul!

Thomas Hood (1799–1845)

3RD OCTOBER

Under the Woods

When these old woods were young
The thrushes' ancestors
As sweetly sung
In the old years.

There was no garden here,
Apples nor mistletoe;
No children dear
Ran to and fro.

New then was this thatched cot,
But the keeper was old,
And he had not
Much lead or gold.

Most silent beech and yew:
As he went round about
The woods to view
Seldom he shot.

But now that he is gone
Out of most memories;
Still lingers on
A stoat of his,

But one, shrivelled and green,
And with no scent at all,
And barely seen
On this shed wall.

Edward Thomas (1878–1917)

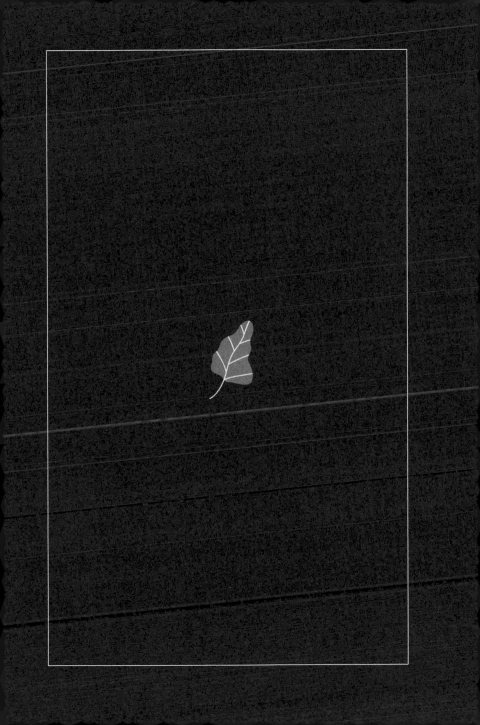

4TH OCTOBER

Autumn's Gold

Along the tops of all the yellow trees,
  The golden-yellow trees, the sunshine lies;
  And where the leaves are gone, long rays surprise
Lone depths of thicket with their brightnesses;
And through the woods, all waste of many a breeze,
  Cometh more joy of light for Poet's eyes –
  Green fields lying yellow underneath the skies,
And shining houses and blue distances.

By the roadside, like rocks of golden ore
  That make the western river-beds so bright,
  The briar and the furze are all alight!
Perhaps the year will be so fair no more,
  But now the fallen, falling leaves are gay,
  And autumn old has shone into a Day!

George MacDonald (1824–1905)

5ᵀᴴ OCTOBER

Grongar Hill

LINES 57–83

Below me trees unnumbered rise,
Beautiful in various dyes:
The gloomy pine, the poplar blue,
The yellow beech, the sable yew,
The slender fir that taper grows,
The sturdy oak, with wide-spread boughs.
And beyond the purple grove,
Haunt of Phillis, queen of love!
Gaudy as the op'ning dawn,
Lies a long and level lawn,
On which a dark hill, steep and high,
Holds and charms the wand'ring eye!
Deep are his feet in Towy's flood,
His sides are cloathed with waving wood,
And ancient towers crown his brow,
That cast an awful look below;
Whose ragged walls the ivy creeps,
And with her arms from falling keeps;
So both a safety from the wind
In mutual dependence find.

'Tis now the raven's bleak abode;
'Tis now th' apartment of the toad;
And there the fox securely feeds;
And there the pois'nous adder breeds,
Concealed in ruins, moss, and weeds;
While, ever and anon, there falls
Huge heap of hoary mouldered walls.

John Dyer (1699–1758)

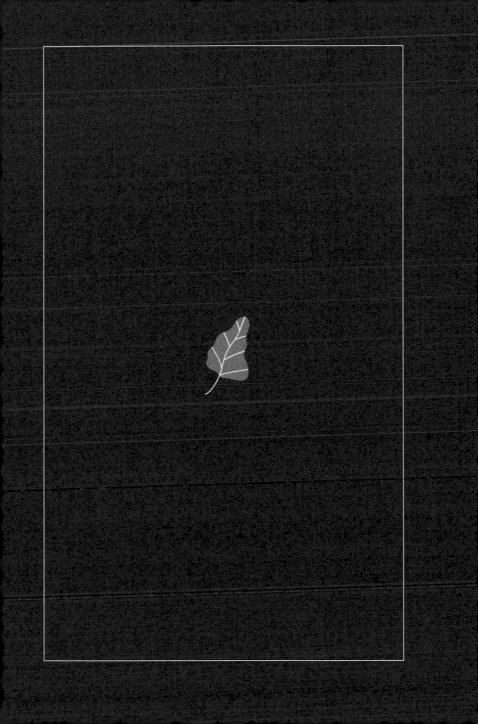

6TH OCTOBER

In Autumn

The leaves are many under my feet,
    And drift one way.
Their scent of death is weary and sweet.
    A flight of them is in the grey
Where sky and forest meet.

The low winds moan for sad sweet years;
    The birds sing all for pain,
Of a common thing, to weary ears, –
    Only a summer's fate of rain,
And a woman's fate of tears.

I walk to love and life alone
    Over these mournful places,
Across the summer overthrown,
    The dead joys of these silent faces,
To claim my own.

I know his heart has beat to bright
    Sweet loves gone by;
I know the leaves that die to-night
    Once budded to the sky;
And I shall die from his delight.

O leaves, so quietly ending now,
    You heard the cuckoos sing.
And I will grow upon my bough
    If only for a Spring,
And fall when the rain is on my brow.

Alice Meynell (1847–1922)

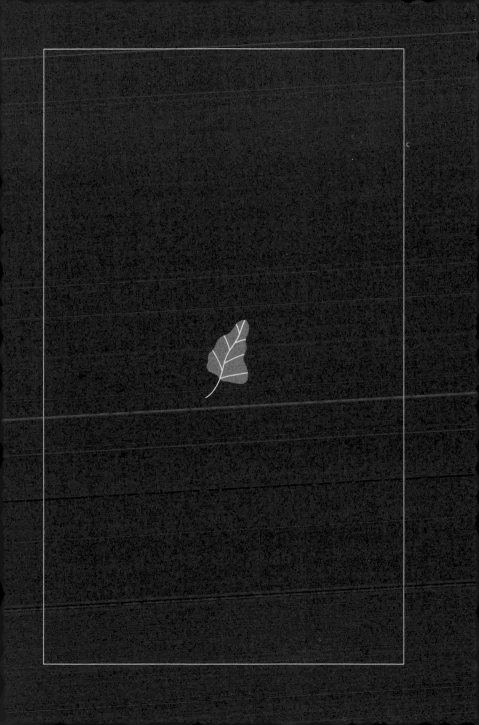

7ᵀᴴ OCTOBER

October

The October water is like glass and scarcely flows.
Beside the red tree the swan spreads a long wing.
Rose hips too are reflected in the stream
Where the bird's sudden movement has made no sound.

Iris Murdoch (1919–1999)

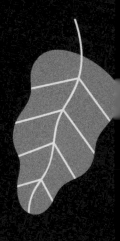

8TH OCTOBER

Flower and Flame

Between the flowering and the flaming woods,
  All greening in the rain,
    The fields unfold;
  The sun upon the grain
    Outpours its gold,
And sweet with bloom and dew are nature's moods
Between the flowering and the flaming woods.

Between the flowering and the flaming woods
  The wind bemoans a host
    Of withered leaves;
  The winter is a ghost
    That grieves and grieves
Around a ruined house where none intrudes,
Between the flaming and the flowering woods.

O woods that break in flower or in flame,
  My wingèd days and hours
    Shall meet their doom
  Like to your leaves and flowers;
    Let not your bloom
And brightness put my flying years to shame.
O woods that break in flower or in flame!

Ethelwyn Wetherald (1857–1940)

9ᵀᴴ OCTOBER

9TH OCTOBER

Astrophil and Stella

With how sad steps, O moon, thou climb'st the skies;
  How silently, and with how wan a face.
  What, may it be that even in heav'nly place
That busy archer his sharp arrows tries?
Sure, if that long-with-love-acquainted eyes
  Can judge of love, thou feel'st a lover's case;
  I read it in thy looks; thy languish'd grace
To me, that feel the like, thy state descries.
  Then, even of fellowship, O moon, tell me,
Is constant love deemed there but want of wit?
Are beauties there as proud as here they be?
Do they above love to be loved, and yet
  Those lovers scorn whom that love doth possess?
  Do they call virtue there ungratefulness?

Sir Philip Sidney (1554–1586)

10ᵀᴴ OCTOBER

God's World

O world, I cannot hold thee close enough!
    Thy winds, thy wide grey skies!
    Thy mists, that roll and rise!
Thy woods, this autumn day, that ache and sag
And all but cry with colour! That gaunt crag
To crush! To lift the lean of that black bluff!
World, World, I cannot get thee close enough!

Long have I known a glory in it all,
    But never knew I this;
    Here such a passion is
As stretcheth me apart, – Lord, I do fear
Thou'st made the world too beautiful this year;
My soul is all but out of me, – let fall
No burning leaf; prithee, let no bird call.

Edna St Vincent Millay (1892–1950)

11ᵀᴴ OCTOBER

A Sunset

Upon the mountain's edge with light touch resting
There a brief while the globe of splendour sits
   And seems a creature of this earth; but soon
    More changeful than the Moon
To wane fantastic his great orb submits.
Or cone or mow of fire: till sinking slowly
Even to a star at length he lessens wholly.

Abrupt, as Spirits vanish, he is sunk!
A soul-like breeze possesses all the wood.
   The boughs, the sprays have stood
As motionless as stands the ancient trunk!
But every leaf through all the forest flutters,
And deep the cavern of the fountain mutters.

Samuel Taylor Coleridge (1772–1834)

12TH OCTOBER

Field of Autumn

Slow moves the acid breath of noon
over the copper-coated hill,
slow from the wild crab's bearded breast
the palsied apples fall.

Like coloured smoke the day hangs fire,
taking the village without sound;
the vulture-headed sun lies low
chained to the violet ground.

The horse upon the rocky height
rolls all the valley in his eye,
but dares not raise his foot or move
his shoulder from the fly.

The sheep, snail-backed against the wall,
lifts her blind face but does not know
the cry her blackened tongue gives forth
is the first bleat of snow.

Each bird and stone, each roof and well
feels the gold foot of autumn pass;
each spider binds with glittering snare
the splintered bones of grass.

Slow moves the hour that sucks our life,
slow drops the late wasp from the pear,
the rose tree's thread of scent draws thin –
and the snaps upon the air.

Laurie Lee (1914–1997)

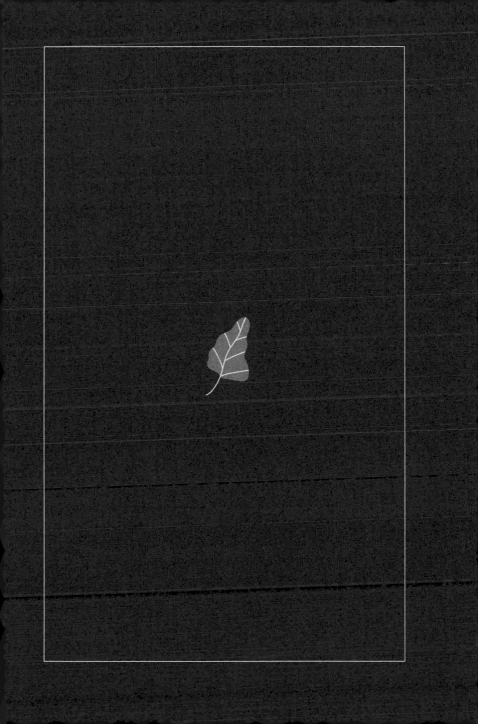

13TH OCTOBER

Beachy Head

LINES 75–84

For now the sun is verging to the sea,
And as he westward sinks, the floating clouds
Suspended, move upon the evening gale,
And gathering round his orb, as if to shade
The insufferable brightness, they resign
Their gauzy whiteness; and more warmed, assume
All hues of purple. There, transparent gold
Mingles with ruby tints, and sapphire gleams,
And colours, such as nature through her works
Shows only in the ethereal canopy.

Charlotte Smith (1749–1806)

14TH OCTOBER

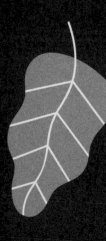

The Secret Strength of Things

MONT BLANC: LINES WRITTEN IN THE VALE OF CHAMOUNI

VERSE I

The everlasting universe of things
Flows through the mind, and rolls its rapid waves,
Now dark, now glittering, now reflecting gloom,
Now lending splendour, where from secret springs
The source of human thought its tribute brings
Of waters – with a sound but half its own,
Such as a feeble brook will oft assume,
In the wild woods, among the mountains lone,
Where waterfalls around it leap for ever,
Where woods and winds contend, and a vast river
Over its rocks ceaselessly bursts and raves.

Percy Bysshe Shelley (1792–1822)

15TH OCTOBER

To the Evening Star

Thou fair-hair'd angel of the evening,
Now, whilst the sun rests on the mountains, light
Thy bright torch of love; thy radiant crown
Put on, and smile upon our evening bed!
Smile on our loves, and while thou drawest the
Blue curtains of the sky, scatter thy silver dew
On every flower that shuts its sweet eyes
In timely sleep. Let thy west wind sleep on
The lake; speak silence with thy glimmering eyes,
And wash the dusk with silver. Soon, full soon,
Dost thou withdraw; then the wolf rages wide,
And then the lion glares through the dun forest:
The fleeces of our flocks are cover'd with
Thy sacred dew: protect them with thine influence.

William Blake (1757–1827)

16TH OCTOBER

The Secret of the Sea

Ah! what pleasant visions haunt me
   As I gaze upon the sea!
All the old romantic legends,
   All my dreams, come back to me.

Sails of silk and ropes of sandal,
   Such as gleam in ancient lore;
And the singing of the sailors,
   And the answer from the shore!

Most of all, the Spanish ballad
   Haunts me oft, and tarries long,
Of the noble Count Arnaldos
   And the sailor's mystic song.

Like the long waves on a sea-beach,
   Where the sand as silver shines,
With a soft, monotonous cadence,
   Flow its unrhymed lyric lines; –

Telling how the Count Arnaldos,
 With his hawk upon his hand,
Saw a fair and stately galley,
 Steering onward to the land; –

How he heard the ancient helmsman
 Chant a song so wild and clear,
That the sailing sea-bird slowly
 Poised upon the mast to hear,

Till his soul was full of longing,
 And he cried, with impulse strong, –
'Helmsman! for the love of heaven,
 Teach me, too, that wondrous song!'

'Wouldst thou,' – so the helmsman answered,
 'Learn the secret of the sea?
Only those who brave its dangers
 Comprehend its mystery!'

In each sail that skims the horizon,
In each landward-blowing breeze,
I behold that stately galley,
Hear those mournful melodies;

Till my soul is full of longing
For the secret of the sea,
And the heart of the great ocean
Sends a thrilling pulse through me.

Henry Wadsworth Longfellow (1807–1882)

17TH OCTOBER

17TH OCTOBER

The Night-Walk

LINES 1–20

Awakes for me and leaps from shroud
All radiantly the moon's own night
Of folded showers in streamer cloud;
Our shadows down the highway white
Or deep in woodland woven-boughed,
With yon and yon a stem alight.

I see marauder runagates
Across us shoot their dusky wink;
I hear the parliament of chats
In haws beside the river's brink;
And drops the vole off alder-banks,
To push his arrow through the stream.
These busy people had our thanks
For tickling sight and sound, but theme
They were not more than breath we drew
Delighted with our world's embrace:
The moss-root smell where beeches grew,
And watered grass in breezy space;
The silken heights, of ghostly bloom
Among their folds, by distance draped.

George Meredith (1828–1909)

18ᵀᴴ OCTOBER

To a Black Greyhound

Shining black in the shining light,
  Inky black in the golden sun,
Graceful as the swallow's flight,
  Light as swallow, wingèd one,
Swift as driven hurricane –
  Double-sinewed stretch and spring,
Muffled thud of flying feet,
  See the black dog galloping,
  Hear his wild foot-beat.

See him lie when the day is dead,
  Black curves curled on the boarded floor.
Sleepy eyes, my sleepy-head –
  Eyes that were aflame before.
Gentle now, they burn no more;
  Gentle now and softly warm,
With the fire that made them bright
  Hidden – as when after storm
  Softly falls the night.

God of speed, who makes the fire –
  God of Peace, who lulls the same –
God who gives the fierce desire,
  Lust for blood as fierce as flame –
God who stands in Pity's name –
  Many may ye be or less,
Ye who rule the earth and sun:
  Gods of strength and gentleness,
  Ye are ever one.

Julian Grenfell (1888–1915)

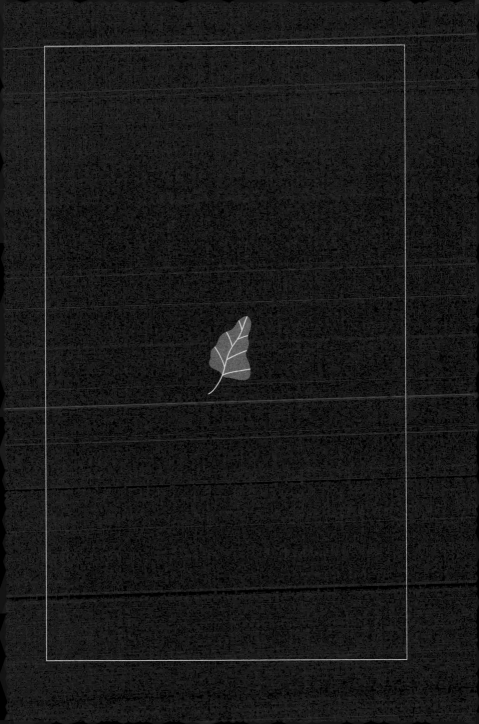

19TH OCTOBER

Silver

Slowly, silently, now the moon
Walks the night in her silver shoon;
This way, and that, she peers, and sees
Silver fruit upon silver trees;
One by one the casements catch
Her beams beneath the silvery thatch;
Couched in his kennel, like a log,
With paws of silver sleeps the dog;
From their shadowy cote the white breasts peep
Of doves in a silver-feathered sleep;
A harvest mouse goes scampering by,
With silver claws, and silver eye;
And moveless fish in the water gleam,
By silver reeds in a silver stream.

Walter de la Mare (1873–1956)

20TH OCTOBER

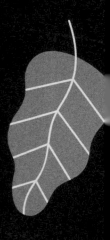

After Rain

See how upon bare twigs they lie,
Raindrops, lately of the sky –
Balls of crystal, rounder far
Than any earthen berries are.
Phantom fruits begot of air
Fashioned for no human fare.

Rachel Field (1894–1942)

21ST OCTOBER

The View

FROM *PROLOGUE TO GENERAL HAMLEY, THE CHARGE OF THE HEAVY BRIGADE AT BALACLAVA*, LINES 1–8

Our birches yellowing and from each
   The light leaf falling fast,
While squirrels from our fiery beech
   Were bearing off the mast,
You came, and look'd and loved the view
   Long-known and loved by me,
Green Sussex fading into blue
   With one gray glimpse of sea.

Alfred, Lord Tennyson (1809–1892)

22ND OCTOBER

Upon the Shore

Who has not walked upon the shore,
And who does not the morning know,
The day the angry gale is o'er,
The hour the wind has ceased to blow?

The horses of the strong southwest
Are pastured round his tropic tent,
Careless how long the ocean's breast
Sob on and sigh for passion spent.

The frightened birds, that fled inland
To house in rock and tower and tree,
Are gathering on the peaceful strand,
To tempt again the sunny sea;

Whereon the timid ships steal out
And laugh to find their foe asleep,
That lately scattered them about,
And drave them to the fold like sheep.

The snow-white clouds he northward chased
Break into phalanx, line, and band:
All one way to the south they haste,
The south, their pleasant fatherland.

From distant hills their shadows creep,
Arrive in turn and mount the lea,
And flit across the downs, and leap
Sheer off the cliff upon the sea;

And sail and sail far out of sight.
But still I watch their fleecy trains,
That piling all the south with light,
Dapple in France the fertile plains.

Robert Bridges (1844–1930)

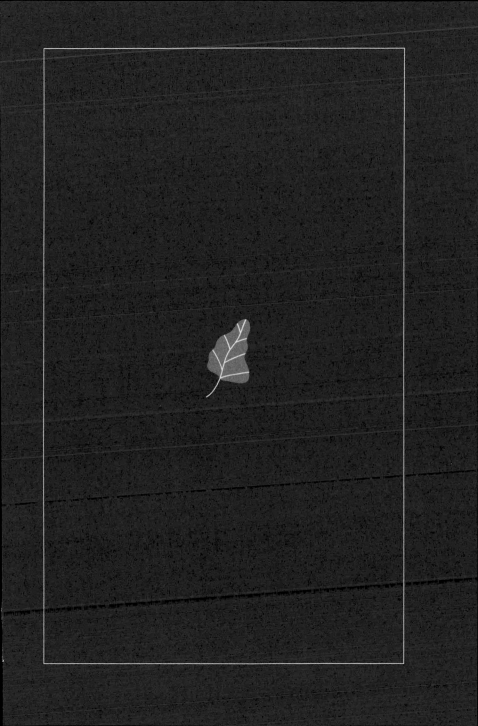

23ᴿᴰ OCTOBER

My Orcha'd in Linden Lea

'Ithin the woodlands, flow'ry gleäded,
　By the woak tree's mossy moot,
The sheenen grass-bleädes, timber-sheäded,
　Now do quiver under voot ;
An' birds do whissle over head,
An' water's bubblen in its bed,
An' there vor me the apple tree
Do leän down low in Linden Lea.

When leaves that leätely wer a-springen
　Now do feäde 'ithin the copse,
An' païnted birds do hush their zingen
　Up upon the timber's tops;
An' brown-leav'd fruit's a-turnen red,
In cloudless zunsheen, over head,
Wi' fruit vor me, the apple tree
Do leän down low in Linden Lea.

Let other vo'k meäke money vaster
　　In the aïr o' dark-room'd towns,
I don't dread a peevish meäster;
　　Though noo man do heed my frowns,
I be free to goo abrode,
Or teäke ageän my homeward road
To where, vor me, the apple tree
Do leän down low in Linden Lea.

William Barnes (1801–1886)

24ᵀᴴ OCTOBER

The Sea-Limits

Consider the sea's listless chime:
   Time's self it is, made audible, –
   The murmur of the earth's own shell.
Secret continuance sublime
   Is the sea's end: our sight may pass
   No furlong further. Since time was,
This sound hath told the lapse of time.

No quiet, which is death's, - it hath
   The mournfulness of ancient life,
   Enduring always at dull strife.
As the world's heart of rest and wrath,
   Its painful pulse is in the sands.
   Last utterly, the whole sky stands,
Grey and not known, along its path.

Listen alone beside the sea,
   Listen alone among the woods;
   Those voices of twin solitudes
Shall have one sound alike to thee:
   Hark where the murmurs of thronged men
   Surge and sink back and surge again, –
Still the one voice of wave and tree.

Gather a shell from the strown beach
  And listen at its lips: they sigh
  The same desire and mystery,
The echo of the whole sea's speech.
  And all mankind is thus at heart
  Not anything but what thou art:
And Earth, Sea, Man, are all in each.

Dante Gabriel Rossetti (1828–1882)

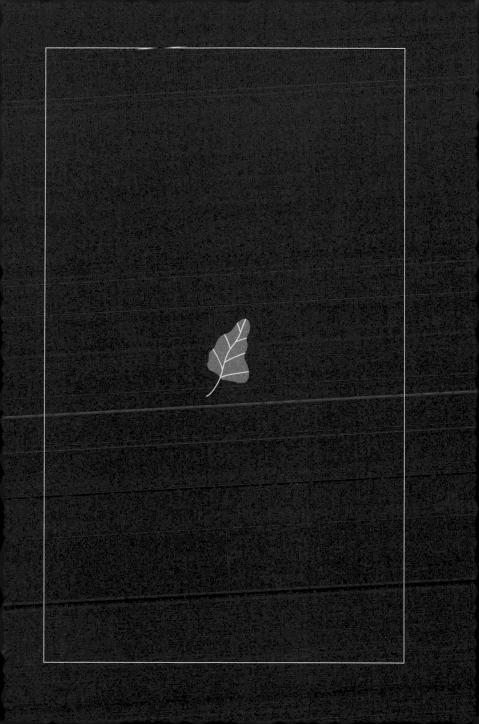

25TH OCTOBER

His Lady's Eyes

FROM *CAELICA*

You little stars that live in skies,
　　And glory in Apollo's glory,
In whose aspects conjoined lies
　　The Heaven's will and Nature's story,
Joy to be likened to those eyes,
　　Which eyes make all eyes glad or sorry;
For when you force thoughts from above,
These overrule your force by love.

And thou, O Love, which in these eyes
　　Hast married Reason with Affection,
And made them saints of Beauty's skies,
Where joys are shadows of perfection,
Lend me thy wings that I may rise
　　Up, not by worth but thy election;
For I have vowed, in strangest fashion
To love and never seek compassion.

Fulke Greville, Lord Brooke (1554–1628)

26TH OCTOBER

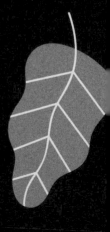

The Birch Tree

Touched with beauty, I stand still and gaze
In the autumn twilight. Yellow leaves and brown
The grass enriching, gleam, or waver down
From lime and elm: far-glimmering through the haze
The quiet lamps in order twinkle; dumb
And fair the park lies; faint the city's hum.

And I regret not June's impassioned prime,
When her deep lilies banqueted the air,
And this now ruined, then so fragrant lime
Cooled with clear green the heavy noon's high glare;
Nor flushed carnations, breathing hot July;
Nor April's thrush in the blithest songs of the year,
With brown bloom on the elms and dazzling sky;
So strange a charm there lingers in this austere
Resigning month, yielding to what must be.
Yet most, O delicate birch, I envy thee,
Child among trees! with silvery slender limbs
And purple sprays of drooping hair. Night dims
The grass; the great elms darken; no birds sing.
At last I sigh for the warmth and the fragrance flown.
But thou in the leafless twilight shinest alone,
Awaiting in ignorant trust the certain spring.

Laurence Binyon (1869–1943)

27TH OCTOBER

The Western Sun Withdraws

FROM *AUTUMN, THE SEASONS*

The western sun withdraws the shorten'd day;
And humid Evening, gliding o'er the sky,
In her chill progress, to the ground condensed
The vapours throws. Where creeping waters ooze,
Where marshes stagnate, and where rivers wind,
Cluster the rolling fogs, and swim along
The dusky-mantled lawn. Meanwhile the moon
Full-orb'd, and breaking through the scatter'd clouds,
Shows her broad visage in the crimson'd east.
Turn'd to the sun direct, her spotted disk,
Where mountains rise, umbrageous dales descend,
And caverns deep, as optic tube descries,
A smaller earth, gives us his blaze again,
Void of its flame, and sheds a softer day.
Now through the passing cloud she seems to stoop,
Now up the pure cerulean rides sublime.
Wide the pale deluge floats, and streaming mild
O'er the sky'd mountain to the shadowy vale,
While rocks and floods reflect the quivering gleam,
The whole air whitens with a boundless tide
Of silver radiance, trembling round the world.

James Thomson (1700–1748)

28TH OCTOBER

Magpies in Picardy

The magpies in Picardy
Are more than I can tell.
They flicker down the dusty roads
And cast a magic spell
On the men who march through Picardy,
Through Picardy to hell.

(The blackbird flies with panic,
The swallow goes like light,
The finches move like ladies,
The owl floats by at night;
But the great and flashing magpie
He flies as artists might.)

A magpie in Picardy
Told me secret things –
Of the music in white feathers,
And the sunlight that sings
And dances in deep shadows –
He told me with his wings.

(The hawk is cruel and rigid,
He watches from a height;
The rook is slow and sombre,
The robin loves to fight;
But the great and flashing magpie
He flies as lovers might.)

He told me that in Picardy,
An age ago or more,
While all his fathers were still eggs,
These dusty highways bore
Brown singing soldiers marching out
Through Picardy to war.

He said that still through chaos
Works on the ancient plan,
And two things have altered not
Since first the world began –
The beauty of the wild green earth
And the bravery of man.

(For the sparrow flies unthinking
And quarrels in his flight;
The heron trails his legs behind,
The lark goes out of sight;
But the great and flashing magpie
He flies as poets might.)

T. P. Cameron Wilson (1891–1918)

29TH OCTOBER

Autumn Birds

The wild duck startles like a sudden thought
And heron slow as if it might be caught
The flopping crows on weary wings go bye
And grey beard jackdaws noising as they flye
The crowds of starnels wiz and hurry bye
And darken like a cloud the evening sky
The larks like thunder rise and suthy round
Then drop and nestle in the stubble ground
The wild swan hurries high and noises loud
With white neck peering to the evening cloud
The weary rooks to distant woods are gone
With length of tail the magpie winnows on
To neighbouring tree, and leaves the distant crow
While small birds nestle in the edge below

John Clare (1793–1864)

30TH OCTOBER

Moonlit Apples

At the top of the house the apples are laid in rows,
And the skylight lets the moonlight in, and those
Apples are deep-sea apples of green. There goes
   A cloud on the moon in the autumn night.

A mouse in the wainscot scratches, and scratches, and then
There is no sound at the top of the house of men
Or mice; and the cloud is blown, and the moon again
   Dapples the apples with deep-sea light.

They are lying in rows there, under the gloomy beams;
On the sagging floor; they gather the silver streams
Out of the moon, those moonlit apples of dreams,
   And quiet is the steep stair under.

In the corridors under there is nothing but sleep.
And stiller than ever on orchard boughs they keep
Tryst with the moon, and deep is the silence, deep
   On moon-washed apples of wonder.

John Drinkwater (1882–1937)

31ˢᵀ OCTOBER

The Fairies

VERSES 1–3

Up the airy mountain,
    Down the rushy glen,
We darent go a-hunting
    For fear of little men;
Wee folk, good folk,
    Trooping all together;
Green jacket, red cap,
    And white owl's feather!

Down along the rocky shore
    Some make their home,
They live on crispy pancakes
    Of yellow tide-foam;
Some in the reeds
    Of the black mountain lake,
With frogs for their watch-dogs,
    All night awake.

High on the hill-top
    The old King sits;
He is now so old and gray
    He's nigh lost his wits.

With a bridge of white mist
  Columbkill he crosses,
On his stately journeys
  From Slieveleague to Rosses;
Or going up with music
  On cold starry nights
To sup with the Queen
  Of the gay Northern Lights.

William Allingham (1824–1889)

NOVEMBER

Starlings Chatter and Chide

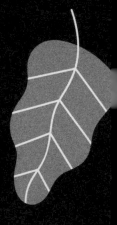

1ST NOVEMBER

Marmion

INTRODUCTION TO CANTO FIRST, LINES 1–36

TO WILLIAM STEWART ROSE, ESQ. ASHESTIEL, ETTRICK
FOREST

November's sky is chill and drear,
November's leaf is red and sear:
Late, gazing down the steepy linn
That hems our little garden in,
Low in its dark and narrow glen
You scarce the rivulet might ken,
So thick the tangled greenwood grew,
So feeble trill'd the streamlet through:
Now, murmuring hoarse, and frequent seen
Through bush and briar, no longer green,
An angry brook, it sweeps the glade,
Brawls over rock and wild cascade,
And foaming brown, with doubled speed,
Hurries its waters to the Tweed.

No longer Autumn's glowing red
Upon our forest hills is shed;
No more, beneath the evening beam,
Fair Tweed reflects their purple gleam:
Away hath passed the heather-bell
That bloom'd so rich on Needpath Fell;

Sallow his brow, and russet bare
Are now the sister-heights of Yair.
The sheep, before the pinching heaven,
To shelter'd dale and down are driven,
Where yet some faded herbage pines,
And yet a watery sunbeam shines:
In meek despondency they eye
The wither'd sward and wintry sky,
And far beneath their summer hill,
Stray sadly by Glenkinnon's rill:
The shepherd shifts his mantle's fold,
And wraps him closer from the cold;
His dogs no merry circles wheel,
But, shivering, follow at his heel;
A cowering glance they often cast,
As deeper moans the gathering blast.

Sir Walter Scott (1771–1832)

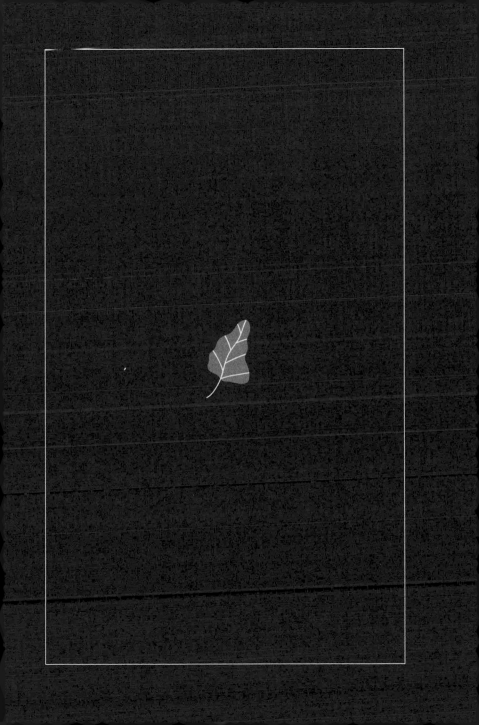

2ND NOVEMBER

The Storm is Over

LINES 1–21

The storm is over, the land hushes to rest:
The tyrannous wind, its strength fordone,
Is fallen back in the west
To couch with the sinking sun.
The last clouds fare
With fainting speed, and their thin streamers fly
In melting drifts of the sky.
Already the birds in the air
Appear again; the rooks return to their haunt,
And one by one,
Proclaiming aloud their care,
Renew their peaceful chant.

Torn and shattered trees their branches again reset,
They trim afresh the fair
Few green and golden leaves withheld from the storm,
And awhile will be handsome yet.
To-morrow's sun shall caress
Their remnant of loveliness:
In quiet days for a time
Sad Autumn lingering warm
Shall humour their faded prime.

Robert Bridges (1844–1930)

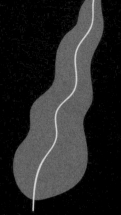

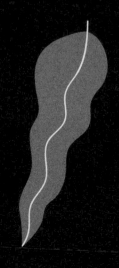

3ʳᵈ NOVEMBER

Echoes

The sea laments
The livelong day,
Fringing its wastes of sand;
Cries back the wind from the whispering shore –
No words I understand:
Yet echoes in my heart a voice,
As far, as near, as these –
The wind that weeps,
The solemn surge
Of strange and lonely seas.

Walter de la Mare (1873–1956)

4TH NOVEMBER

The Last Robin

The spring was red with robins,
  The summer gay with their song;
What doest thou here at the bleak of the year,
  When the frost is sharp and strong,
When even the red from the leaves has fled,
  And the stormy night is long?

Silent, alone, thou givest
  An April gleam to the lane;
A sense of spring to the sorrowing
  Of autumn wind and rain.
Dear gleam, good-bye! the dark is nigh;
  Good-bye – come back again!

Ethelwyn Wetherald (1857–1940)

5TH NOVEMBER

Beachy Head

LINES 368–389

Ah! hills so early loved! in fancy still
I breathe your pure keen air; and still behold
Those widely spreading views, mocking alike
The poet and the painter's utmost art.
And still, observing objects more minute,
Wondering remark the strange and foreign forms
Of seashells; with the pale calcareous soil
Mingled, and seeming of resembling substance.
Tho' surely the blue ocean 'from the heights
Where the Downs westward trend, but dimly seen'
Here never rolled its surge. Does nature then
Mimic, in wanton mood, fantastic shapes
Of bivalves, and inwreathed volutes, that cling
To the dark sea-rock of the wat'ry world?
Or did this range of chalky mountains, once
Form a vast basin, where the ocean waves
Swelled fathomless? What time these fossil shells,
Buoyed on their native element, were thrown
Among the imbedding calx: when the huge hill
Its giant bulk heaved, and in strange ferment
Grew up a guardian barrier, 'twixt the sea
And the green level of the sylvan weald.

Charlotte Smith (1749–1806)

6TH NOVEMBER

November

Are thine eyes weary? is thy heart too sick
To struggle any more with doubt and thought,
Whose formless veil draws darkening now and thick
Across thee, e'en as smoke-tinged mist-wreaths brought
Down a fair dale to make it blind and nought?
Art thou so weary that no world there seems
Beyond these four walls, hung with pain and dreams?

Look out upon the real world, where the moon,
Half-way 'twixt root and crown of these high trees,
Turns the dead midnight into dreamy noon,
Silent and full of wonders, for the breeze
Died at the sunset, and no images,
No hopes of day, are left in sky or earth –
Is it not fair, and of most wondrous worth?

Yea, I have looked, and seen November there;
The changeless seal of change it seemed to be,
Fair death of things that, living once, were fair;
Bright sign of loneliness too great for me,
Strange image of the dread eternity,
In whose void patience how can these have part,
These outstretched feverish hands, this restless heart?

William Morris (1834–1896)

7ᵀᴴ NOVEMBER

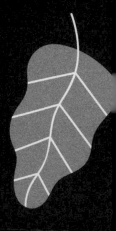

Stars

Alone in the night
  On a dark hill
With pines around me
  Spicy and still,

And a heaven full of stars
  Over my head
White and topaz
  And misty red;

Myriads with beating
  Hearts of fire
That aeons
  Cannot vex or tire;

Up the dome of heaven
  Like a great hill
I watch them marching
  Stately and still.

And I know that I
  Am honored to be
Witness
  Of so much majesty.

Sara Teasdale (1884–1933)

8ᵀᴴ NOVEMBER

Autumn

1

I love the fitfull gusts that shakes
   The casement all the day
And from the glossy elm tree takes
   The faded leaf away
Twirling it by the window pane
With thousand others down the lane

2

I love to see the shaking twig
   Dance till the shut of eve
The sparrow on the cottage rig
   Whose chirp would make believe
That spring was just now flirting by
In summers lap with flowers to lie

3

I love to see the cottage smoke
   Curl upwards through the naked trees
The pigeons nestled round the coat
   On dull november days like these
The cock upon the dunghill crowing
The mill sails on the heath agoing

4

The feather from the ravens breast
  Falls on the stubble lea
The acorns near the old crows nest
  Fall pattering down the tree
The grunting pigs that wait for all
Scramble and hurry where they fall

John Clare (1793-1864)

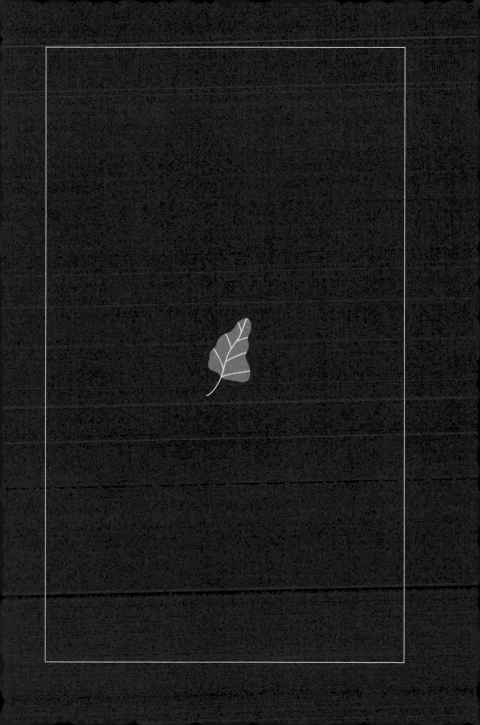

9TH NOVEMBER

Childe Harold's Pilgrimage

CANTO THE THIRD

LXXXVIII

Ye stars! which are the poetry of heaven
If in your bright leaves we would read the fate
Of men and empires, – 'tis to be forgiven,
That in our aspirations to be great,
Our destinies o'erleap their mortal state,
And claim a kindred with you; for ye are
A beauty and mystery, and create
In us such love and reverence from afar,
That fortune, fame, power, life, have named themselves a star.

LXXXIX

All heaven and earth are still – though not in sleep,
But breathless, as we grow when feeling most;
And silent, as we stand in thoughts too deep: –
All heaven and earth are still: From the high host
Of stars, to the lull'd lake and mountain-coast,
All is concenter'd in a life intense,
Where not a beam, nor air, nor leaf is lost,
But hath a part of being, and a sense
Of that which is of all Creator and defence.

George Gordon, Lord Byron (1788–1824)

10TH NOVEMBER

Gradual Clearing

Late in the day the fog
wrung itself out like a sponge
in glades of rain,
sieving the half-invisible
cove with speartips;
then, in a lifting
of wisps and scarves, of smoke-rings
from about the islands, disclosing
what had been wavering
fishnet plissé as a smoothness
of peau-de-soie or just-ironed
percale, with a tatting
of foam out where the rocks are,
the sheened no-color of it,
the bandings of platinum
and magnesium suffusing,
minute by minute, with clandestine
rose and violet, with opaline
nuance of milkweed, a texture
not to be spoken of above a whisper,
began, all along the horizon,
gradually to unseal
like the lip of a cave
or of a cavernous,
single, pearl-
engendering seashell.

Amy Clampitt (1920–1994)

11TH NOVEMBER

A Hymn in Praise of Neptune

Of Neptune's empire let us sing,
At whose command the waves obey,
To whom the rivers tribute pay,
　　Down the high mountains sliding;
To whom the scaly nation yields
Homage for the crystal fields
　　　　Wherein they dwell;
And every sea-god pays a gem,
Yearly out of his watery cell,
To deck the great Neptune's diadem.

The Tritons dancing in a ring
Before his palace gates, do make
The water with their echoes quake,
　　Like the great thunder sounding:
The sea-nymphs chant their accents shrill;
　　And the Sirens, taught to kill
　　　　With their sweet voice,
Make every echoing rock reply
Unto their gentle murmuring noise
The praise of Neptune's empery.

Thomas Campion (1567–1620)

12TH NOVEMBER

The Parrot

TRANSLATED BY WILLIAM COWPER

In painted plumes superbly drest,
A native of the gorgeous east,
　　By many a billow tost;
Poll gains at length the British shore,
Part of the captain's precious store –
　　A present to his toast.

Belinda's maids are soon preferr'd,
To teach him now then a word,
　　As Poll can master it;
But 'tis her own important charge,
To qualify him more at large,
　　And make him quite a wit.

Sweet Poll! his doating mistress cries,
Sweet Poll! the mimic bird replies,
　　And calls aloud for sack.
She next instructs him in the kiss;
'Tis now a little one, like Miss,
　　And now a hearty smack.

At first he aims at what he hears;
And, list'ning close with both his ears,
   Just catches at the sound;
But soon articulates aloud,
Much to th' amusement of the crowd,
   And stuns the neighbours round.

A querulous old woman's voice
His hum'rous talent next employs –
   He scolds and gives the lie.
And now he sings, and now is sick –
Here, Sally, Susan, come, come quick,
   Poor Poll is like to die!

Belinda and her bird! 'tis rare
To meet with such a well match'd pair,
   The language and the tone,
Each character in ev'ry part
Sustain'd with so much grace and art,
   And both in unison.

When children first begin to spell,
And stammer out a syllable,
   We think them tedious creatures;
But difficulties soon abate,
When birds are to be taught to prate,
   And women are the teachers.

Vincent Bourne (1695–1747)

13TH NOVEMBER

The Moon

She comes! again she comes, the bright-eyed moon!
Under a ragged cloud I found her out,
Clasping her own dark orb like hope in doubt!
That ragged cloud hath waited her since noon,
And he hath found and he will hide her soon!
Come, all ye little winds that sit without,
And blow the shining leaves her edge about,
And hold her fast – ye have a pleasant tune!
She will forget us in her walks at night
Among the other worlds that are so fair!
She will forget to look on our despair!
She will forget to be so young and bright!
Nay, gentle moon, thou hast the keys of light –
I saw them hanging by thy girdle there!

George MacDonald (1824–1905)

14TH NOVEMBER

Hayeswater Boat

VERSES 1 AND 2

A region desolate and wild.
Black, chafing water: and afloat,
And lonely as a truant child
In a waste wood, a single boat:
No mast, no sails are set thereon;
It moves, but never moveth on:
And welters like a human thing
Amid the wild waves weltering.

Behind, a buried vale doth sleep,
Far down the torrent cleaves its way:
In front the dumb rock rises steep,
A fretted wall of blue and grey;
Of shooting cliff and crumbled stone
With many a wild weed overgrown:
All else, black water: and afloat,
One rood from shore, that single boat.

Matthew Arnold (1822–1888)

15TH NOVEMBER

At a Lunar Eclipse

Thy shadow, Earth, from Pole to Central Sea,
Now steals along upon the Moon's meek shine
In even monochrome and curving line
Of imperturbable serenity.

How shall I link such sun-cast symmetry
With the torn troubled form I know as thine,
That profile, placid as a brow divine,
With continents of moil and misery?

And can immense Mortality but throw
So small a shade, and Heaven's high human scheme
Be hemmed within the coasts yon arc implies?

Is such the stellar gauge of earthly show,
Nation at war with nation, brains that teem,
Heroes, and women fairer than the skies?

Thomas Hardy (1840–1928)

16TH NOVEMBER

On Rover, A Lady's Spaniel

ADVICE TO A DOG PAINTER, LINES 1–16

Happiest of the spaniel race,
Painter, with thy colours grace:
Draw his forehead large and high,
Draw his blue and humid eye;
Draw his neck so smooth and round,
Little neck with ribbons bound,
And the muscly swelling breast,
Where the Loves and Graces rest;
And the spreading, even back,
Soft, and sleek, and glossy black;
And the tail that gently twines,
Like the tendrils of the vines;
And the silky twisted hair,
Shadowing thick the velvet ear;
Velvet ears, which, hanging low,
O'er the veiny temples flow.

Jonathan Swift (1667–1745)

17TH NOVEMBER

November

The lonely season in lonely lands, when fled
Are half the birds, and mists lie low, and the sun
Is rarely seen, nor strayeth far from his bed;
The short days pass unwelcomed one by one.

  Out by the ricks the mantled engine stands
Crestfallen, deserted, – for now all hands
Are told to the plough, – and ere it is dawn appear
The teams following and crossing far and near,
As hour by hour they broaden the brown bands
Of the striped fields; and behind them firk and prance
The heavy rooks, and daws grey-pated dance:
As awhile, surmounting a crest, in sharp outline
(A miniature of toil, a gem's design,)
They are pictured, horses and men, or now near by
Above the lane they shout lifting the share,
By the trim hedgerow bloom'd with purple air;
Where, under the thorns, dead leaves in huddle lie
Packed by the gales of Autumn, and in and out
The small wrens glide
With a happy note of cheer,
And yellow amorets flutter above and about,
Gay, familiar in fear.

And now, if the night shall be cold, across the sky
Linnets and twites, in small flocks helter-skelter,
All the afternoon to the gardens fly,
From thistle-pastures hurrying to gain the shelter
Of American rhododendron or cherry-laurel:
And here and there, near chilly setting of sun,
In an isolated tree a congregation
Of starlings chatter and chide,
Thickset as summer leaves, in garrulous quarrel:
Suddenly they hush as one, –
The tree top springs, –
And off, with a whirr of wings,
They fly by the score

To the holly-thicket, and there with myriads more
Dispute for the roosts; and from the unseen nation
A babel of tongues, like running water unceasing,
Makes live the wood, the flocking cries increasing,
Wrangling discordantly, incessantly,
While falls the night on them self-occupied;
The long dark night, that lengthens slow,
Deepening with Winter to starve grass and tree,
And soon to bury in snow
The Earth, that, sleeping 'neath her frozen stole,
Shall dream a dream crept from the sunless pole
Of how her end shall be.

Robert Bridges (1844–1930)

18TH NOVEMBER

By the Sea

Why does the sea moan evermore?
   Shut out from heaven it makes its moan,
It frets against the boundary shore;
   All earth's full rivers cannot fill
   The sea, that drinking thirsteth still.

Sheer miracles of loveliness
   Lie hid in its unlooked-on bed:
Anemones, salt, passionless,
   Blow flower-like; just enough alive
   To blow and multiply and thrive.

Shells quaint with curve, or spot, or spike,
   Encrusted live things argus-eyed,
All fair alike, yet all unlike,
   Are born without a pang, and die
   Without a pang, and so pass by.

Christina Rossetti (1830–1894)

19TH NOVEMBER

To Night

I

Swiftly walk o'er the western wave,
    Spirit of Night!
Out of the misty eastern cave,
Where, all the long and lone daylight,
Thou wovest dreams of joy and fear,
Which make thee terrible and dear, –
    Swift be thy flight!

II

Wrap thy form in a mantle gray,
    Star-inwrought!
Blind with thine hair the eyes of Day;
Kiss her until she be wearied out,
Then wander o'er city, and sea, and land,
Touching all with thine opiate wand –
    Come, long-sought!

III

When I arose and saw the dawn
    I sighed for thee;
When light rode high, and the dew was gone,
And noon lay heavy on flower and tree,
And the weary Day turned to his rest,
Lingering like an unloved guest.
    I sighed for thee.

Percy Bysshe Shelley (1792–1822)

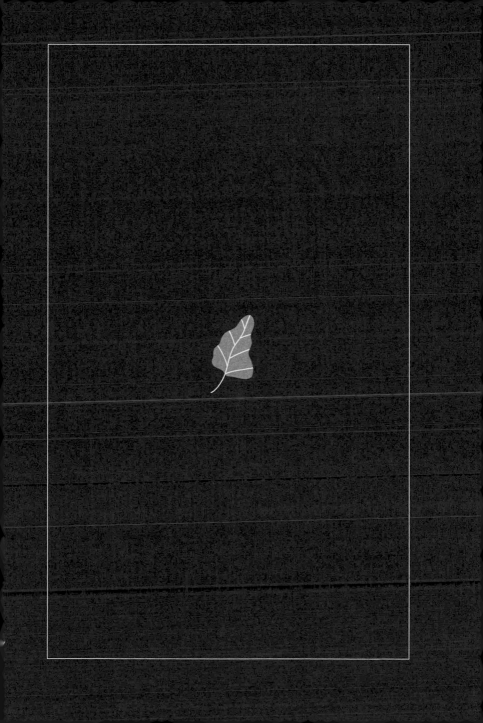

20TH NOVEMBER

To Flush, My Dog

Loving friend, the gift of one,
Who, her own true faith, hath run,
Through thy lower nature;
Be my benediction said
With my hand upon thy head,
Gentle fellow-creature!

Like a lady's ringlets brown,
Flow thy silken ears adown
Either side demurely,
Of thy silver-suited breast
Shining out from all the rest
Of thy body purely.

Darkly brown thy body is,
Till the sunshine, striking this,
Alchemize its dulness, -
When the sleek curls manifold
Flash all over into gold,
With a burnished fulness.

Underneath my stroking hand,
Startled eyes of hazel bland
Kindling, growing larger, -
Up thou leapest with a spring,
Full of prank and curvetting,
Leaping like a charger.

Leap! thy broad tail waves a light ;
Leap! thy slender feet are bright,
Canopied in fringes.
Leap - those tasselled ears of thine
Flicker strangely, fair and fine,
Down their golden inches

Yet, my pretty sportive friend,
Little is't to such an end
That I praise thy rareness!
Other dogs may be thy peers
Haply in these drooping ears,
And this glossy fairness.

But of thee it shall be said,
This dog watched beside a bed
Day and night unweary, -
Watched within a curtained room,
Where no sunbeam brake the gloom
Round the sick and dreary.

Roses, gathered for a vase,
In that chamber died apace,
Beam and breeze resigning -
This dog only, waited on,
Knowing that when light is gone,
Love remains for shining.

Elizabeth Barrett Browning (1806-1861)

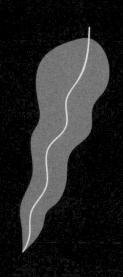

21ˢᵀ NOVEMBER

The Tuft of Kelp

All dripping in tangles green,
  Cast up by a lonely sea
If purer for that, O Weed,
  Bitterer, too, are ye?

Herman Melville (1819–1891)

22ND NOVEMBER

The Shell

What has the sea swept up?
A Viking oar, long mouldered in the peace
Of grey oblivion? Some dim-burning bowl
Of unmixed gold, from far-off island feasts?
Ropes of old pearls? Masses of ambergris?
Something of elfdom from the ghastly isles
Where white-hot rocks pierce through the flying spindrift?
Or a pale sea-queen, close wound in a net of spells?

Nothing of these. Nothing of antique splendours
That have a weariness about their names:
But – fresh and new, in frail transparency,
Pink as a baby's nail, silky and veined
As a flower petal – this casket of the sea,
One shell.

Mary Webb (1881–1927)

23ᴿᴰ NOVEMBER

Escape at Bedtime

The lights from the parlour and kitchen shone out
  Through the blinds and the windows and bars;
And high overhead and all moving about,
  There were thousands of millions of stars.
There ne'er were such thousands of leaves on a tree,
  Nor of people in church or the Park,
As the crowds of the stars that looked down upon me,
  And that glittered and winked in the dark.

The Dog, and the Plough, and the Hunter, and all,
  And the star of the sailor, and Mars,
These shone in the sky, and the pail by the wall
  Would be half full of water and stars.
They saw me at last, and they chased me with cries,
  And they soon had me packed into bed;
But the glory kept shining and bright in my eyes,
  And the stars going round in my head.

Robert Louis Stevenson (1850–1894)

24TH NOVEMBER

Inversnaid

This dárksome búrn, hórseback brówn,
His rollrock highroad roaring down,
In coop and in comb the fleece of his foam
Flutes and low to the lake falls home.

A wíndpuff-bónnet of fáwn-fróth
Turns and twindles over the broth
Of a póol so pítchblack, féll-frówning,
It rounds and rounds Despair to drowning.

Degged with dew, dappled with dew
And the groins of the braes that the brook treads through,
Wiry heathpacks, flitches of fern,
And the beadbonny ash that sits over the burn.

What would the world be, once bereft
Of wet and of wildness? Let them be left,
O let them be left, wildness and wet;
Long live the weeds and the wilderness yet.

Gerard Manley Hopkins (1844–1889)

25TH NOVEMBER

Twilight

The stately tragedy of dusk
  Drew to its perfect close,
The virginal white evening star
  Sank and the red moon rose.

Sara Teasdale (1884–1933)

26TH NOVEMBER

Gulf

with pale determination we stood either
side of the gulf, hair quite salt-
stung, a metallic taste in our mouths.

breath poised.

then the gulf widened, its perimeter
was lost & into that breach
poured the wind: a night wind that could
not recall day's passing.

Joel Knight (1975–)

27TH NOVEMBER

The Last Walk in Autumn

VERSES 1–3

I

O'er the bare woods, whose outstretched hands
    Plead with the leaden heavens in vain,
I see, beyond the valley lands,
    The sea's long level dim with rain.
Around me all things, stark and dumb,
    Seem praying for the snows to come,
And, for the summer bloom and greenness gone,
With winter's sunset lights and dazzling morn atone.

II

Along the river's summer walk,
    The withered tufts of asters nod;
And trembles on its arid stalk
    The boar plume of the golden-rod.
And on a ground of sombre fir,
    And azure-studded juniper,
The silver birch its buds of purple shows,
And scarlet berries tell where bloomed the sweet wild-rose!

III

With mingled sound of horns and bells,
   A far-heard clang, the wild geese fly,
Storm-sent, from Arctic moors and fells,
   Like a great arrow through the sky,
Two dusky lines converged in one,
   Chasing the southward-flying sun;
While the brave snow-bird and the hardy jay
Call to them from the pines, as if to bid them stay.

John Greenleaf Whittier (1807–1892)

28ᵀᴴ NOVEMBER

The Cormorant

Now the seagull spreads his wing,
And the puffin seeks the shore,
Home flies every living thing,
Yo, ho! the breakers roar!
  Only the Cormorant, dark and sly,
  Watches the waves with a sea-green eye.

Under his bows the breakers fleet,
All alone, alone went he;
Flying alone through the blinding sleet.
Flying alone through the raging sea.
  Only the Cormorant, dark and sly,
  Watches the waves with a sea-green eye.

Round his bark the billows roar,
Dancing along to a lonely grave;
Death behind, and Death before
Yo, ho! the breakers rave!
  Only the Cormorant, dark and sly,
  Watches the waves with a sea-green eye.

Hark! the waves on their iron floor,
See Kilstiffin's naked brow!
Iron cliff, and iron shore,
Erin's saints preserve him now!
  Only the Cormorant, dark and sly,
  Watches the waves with a sea-green eye.

Hark! was that a drowing cry?
Erin's saints receive his soul!
Nothing now twixt sea and sky
Yo, ho! the breakers roll!
  Only the Cormorant, dark and sly,
  Watches the waves with a sea-green eye.

Emily Lawless (1845–1913)

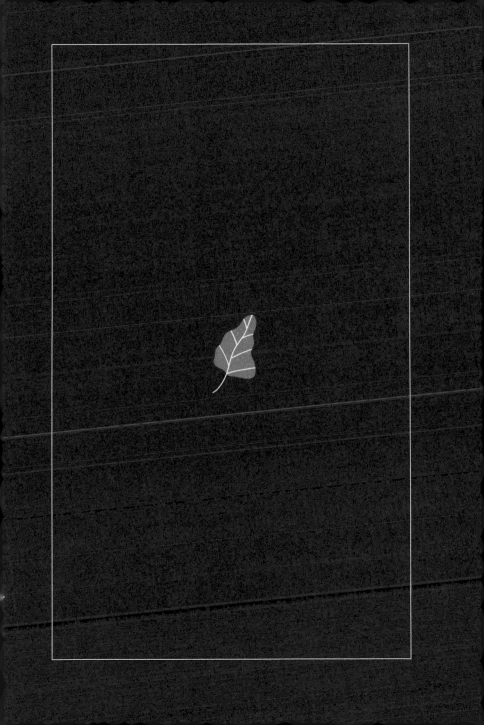

29TH NOVEMBER

A Winter Piece

The time has been that these wild solitudes,
Yet beautiful as wild – were trod by me
Oftener than now; and when the ills of life
Had chafed my spirit – when the unsteady pulse
Beat with strange flutterings – I would wander forth
And seek the woods. The sunshine on my path
Was to me as a friend. The swelling hills,
The quiet dells retiring far between,
With gentle invitation to explore
Their windings, were a calm society
That talked with me and soothed me. Then the chant
Of birds, and chime of brooks, and soft caress
Of the fresh sylvan air, made me forget
The thoughts that broke my peace, and I began
To gather simples by the fountain's brink,
And lose myself in day-dreams. While I stood
In nature's loneliness, I was with one
With whom I early grew familiar, one
Who never had a frown for me, whose voice
Never rebuked me for the hours I stole
From cares I loved not, but of which the world
Deems highest, to converse with her. When shrieked
The bleak November winds, and smote the woods,

And the brown fields were herbless, and the shades,
That met above the merry rivulet,
Were spoiled, I sought, I loved them still, – they seemed
Like old companions in adversity.

William Cullen Bryant (1794–1878)

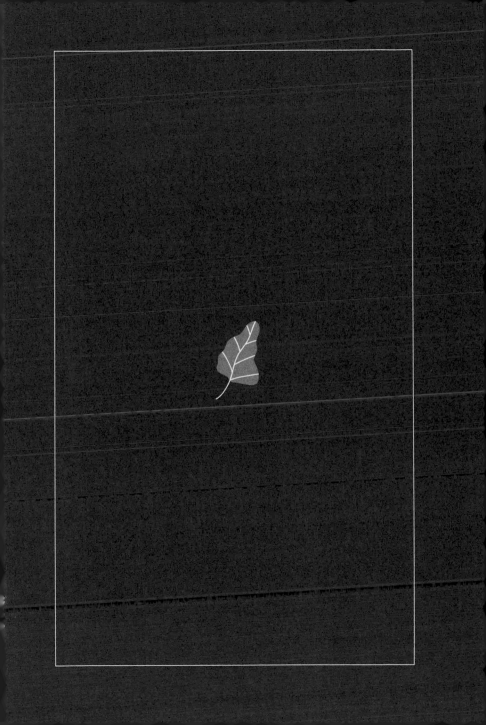

30TH NOVEMBER

Written in November

Autumn I love thy latter end to view
In cold Novembers day so bleak and bare
When like lifes dwindld thread worn nearly thro
Wi lingering pottering pace and head bleached bare
Thou like an old man bids the world adieu
I love thee well and often as a child
Have roamd the bare brown heath a flower to find
And in the moss clad vale and wood bank wild
Have cropt the little bell flowers paley blue
That trembling peept the sheltering bush behind
When winnowing north winds cold and blealy blew
How I have joyd wi dithering hands to findd
Each fading flower and still how sweet the blast
Would bleak novembers hour Restore the joy thats past

John Clare (1793–1864)

Index of first lines

Index of poets

Acknowledgements

As always, a huge thanks to everyone at Hatchards in Piccadilly, St Pancras and Cheltenham for looking after my books so well.

Thanks to all my friends who made recommendations, and Nicola Newman and Magda Simões-Brown, my wonderful editors at Batsford.

For curious readers, Matilda is a small grey tabby cat who went missing in late autumn when I was compiling the original anthology from which this collection is taken. By spring she had been rescued and resumed her duties as paperweight but without Mat and Sarah it would have been a much harder time.

Sources

John Betjeman, 'Diary of a Church Mouse', from *John Betjeman Collected Poems*, John Murray Press. an imprint of Hodder and Stoughton Limited.

Walter de la Mare, 'Silver', from *Walter de la Mare Selected Poems*, Faber & Faber, 2006. 'Echoes', from Collected Rhymes and Verses, Faber & Faber, 1944. Courtesy of The Literary Trustees of Walter de la Mare and the Society of Authors as their Representative.

Robert Frost, 'The Road Not Taken', from *The Complete Poems*, Cape, 1951, Penguin Random House.

Ted Hughes, 'The Harvest Moon', from *New Selected Poems 1957-1994*, Faber & Faber Ltd, 1995.

Joel Knight, 'Gulf'. With kind permission of Joel Knight.

Laurie Lee, 'Field of Autumn', from *Poets of Our Time*, J. Murray, 1965, Penguin Random House.

Iris Murdoch, 'October', from *A Year of Birds*, Chatto & Windus, 1984, Penguin Random House.

Vita Sackville-West, 'Autumn', from *The Land*, Francis Lincoln, 1989, Penguin Random House.